This book is dedicated
to my Dad.
Love,
Todd

First published 2000 by
Little, Brown and Company, USA

First published in Great Britain 2001
by Walker Books Ltd
87 Vauxhall Walk, London SE11 5HJ

2 4 6 8 10 9 7 5 3 1

© 2000 Todd Parr

Printed in Hong Kong

British Library Cataloguing in Publication Data:
a catalogue record for this book
is available from the British Library

ISBN 0-7445-9221-6

UNDERWEAR
Do's and Don'ts

Todd PARR

WALKER BOOKS
AND SUBSIDIARIES
LONDON • BOSTON • SYDNEY

DO

Have lots of different kinds of underwear

Do

Wash your underwear

Don't

Put it in the freezer

Don't

Let her try it on

RRIP

Do

Dress up your dog in underwear

DO

Wear fancy underwear under your dress

Hang upside down on the monkey bars

Give cool underwear as a present

Do

Go swimming in
your underwear

Don't

Jump off the diving board

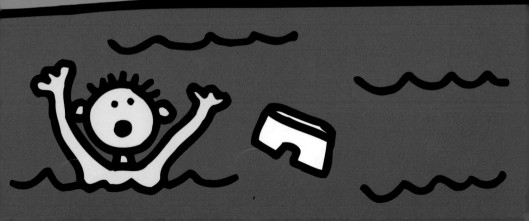

Do

Give striped
underwear
to a zebra

Give him
polka-dotted
ones